SIPPS Plus

Dreams on Wheels
and other selections

Third Edition

Contents

A Pet? 1

A Pet Rat? 4

What Is It? 7

Ants 10

In the Web 12

Six a.m. to Ten p.m 15

Set Up a Fish Tank 18

A Wish 22

The Fox and the Hen 25

Bird Bills 28

The Dog Guide, Part 1: Ron and Lab 31

The Dog Guide, Part 2: To Ron's Job 34

The Dog Guide, Part 3: Lab, the Pet 37

My Motorcycles 39

Of Dogs and Men: Two Fables 42

Birds That Can't Fly, Part 1: The Penguin 44

Birds That Can't Fly, Part 2: The Ostrich 47

Birds That Can't Fly, Part 3: Compare Penguins
    and Ostriches 51

In the States, Part 1: The USA, by Pete 53

In the States, Part 2: The USA, by Ann 57

My Fine Kids 61

Camping Trip 64

Hang Gliding 68

Using Smell 71

Earthquakes 74

Leeches 77

continues

Contents *continued*

Dreams on Wheels 80
First Plane to Fly 83
The Big Games. 86
Sunset with the Herd 91
Jobs in Parks. 95
Firefighters. 99
Job Hunt 103
Stagehand. 107
Vampire Bats 110
Soccer or Football?. 114
Talking with a Go-kart Racer. 118
Floating Down Rivers 122
Dams, Part 1: Why Dams Are Built. 126
Dams, Part 2: How Dams Are Built. 129
The Daily Mouse 132
Neighbors. 138
Photos. 142
Laughing. 147
Country Farming and City Farming 152
Life in Antarctica. 156
Lost. 161
Dress Codes 166
Mountain Lions 170
The Race to the South Pole. 175

A Pet?

cricket

boa constrictor

tarantula spider

lizard

"Is it as big as a dog?"
        "No, it is not."

"Is it as big as a cat?"
        "No."

"Is it as big as my hand?"
        "No, it is not."

"Can it sit on my lap?"
        "Yes, it can."

"Can it fit in a big sack?"
        "Yes."

"Will it sit on a rock?"
        "Yes, it can."

"Can it go fast?"
        "Not so fast."

"Can it hop?"
        "Yes, it can."

"Will it hop on your back?"
        "Yes, it will."

"Is it black?"
            "Yes and no."

"Is it as big as a rat?"
            "No."

"Will your mom pet it?
            "No!"

"Does it get wet a lot?
            "No, it does not."

"Can it go down your leg?"
            "Yes."

"Can it sit on your neck?"
            "Yes."

"Does it go in your bed?"
            "Not in my bed!"

What will you ask?

What is it?

A Pet Rat?

I want a pet. But I can not get a cat. I can not get a dog.

What? A rat! A rat is not a pet. A rat is bad. It can run under my bed. It can rip up the rug. It can mess up my van.

A pet rat can live in a tin box if you fix it up. You can mix up food in a tin can and set the can in the box. If a sack is in the box, the rat will rip it up to have a bed.

A rat will run and run and run.

A rat can sit on your lap. It will run up your back and sit on your neck.

People will not want to sit next to you and your rat. If you go on the bus, have the rat sit under your hat.

Will the man get the pet rat? Why? Why not?

What Is It?

black widow spider

Gila monster lizard

rattlesnake

fire ants

"If you are bit, will you get sick?"
      "Yes, you will."

"Can it kill you?"
      "Yes."

"Will it be bad if you are a kid?"
      "Yes, it will be."

"Where does it live? Can it get you at your job?"
      "Yes and no."

"Can it live where it is hot?"
      "Yes, it can."

"If a man is bit, can he get help?"
      "Yes, he can."

"Can my mom get help?"
      "Yes, she can."

"Does she have to act fast?"
          "Yes, she does."

"Do a lot live by us?"
          "Yes and no."

"If I am bit by just one, can it kill me?"
          "Yes."

"Is it all black?"
          "No."

"Can one be under the edge of a rock?"
          "Yes."

"Can one be on the edge of a log?"
          "Yes, it can."

"Can it buzz?"
          "No. It can not buzz."

What will you ask next?

What is it?

Ants

All ants have six legs. Some ants are black. Some are red. Some are tan.

Ants live in an ant nest. The nest can be a hill. The nest can be in a log. Ants can live in a wall. One nest has many, many ants, up to 8,000,000.

Some ants are small, but they can kill a big bug. They can pick it up and get it back to the nest.

Fire ants can be bad. They get mad if you dig in the nest. Many ants come from the nest. The nest has so many ants on it, it gets black. The ants go up your sock and up your leg. You will be bit, and you can get sick. If a buck is bit by many fire ants, it will not live.

buck

In the Web

garden spider

Many bugs have six legs. An ant has six legs. But all spiders have 8 legs.

Spiders have poison. It can help get bugs.

Many spiders get bugs in a silk web. The spider will sit at the edge of the web. If a bug hits the web, the bug will get stuck. The spider will run to the bug. It will put poison in the bug. Next, it will put the bug in silk. If the bug rips the web, the spider has to fix the web and go back to the edge.

daddy long legs spider in a web

black widow spider

Some spiders can poison people. The black widow is one. It has a red spot on it. But people will not get bit by most spiders. Most spiders can not cut the skin of people.

Most people do not want to sit by a spider. But spiders help us. They kill many, many bugs.

Six a.m. to Ten p.m.

The customer thinks, "I can go in from six a.m. to ten p.m. I can stop on my way. If I stop in my van, I can get gas. If I am lost, they have a map."

The family thinks, "This is an all-day job. At six a.m. men come in for a hot drink. Then at 12:00 we sell a lot of hot dogs.

"At 3:00 kids come in for gum, pop, nuts, and snacks. Then at 5:00 we sell a lot of milk."

All day we say, "Can I help you? . . . What will you have? . . . Is that all? . . . I will add it up. . . . That will be $6.95. . . . Thank you. . . . I will put this in a bag. . . . Next."

Stock is what we sell. At ten p.m. we have to get the stock out and set it up. We put up the ads. Then we have to pick up and mop. That is the end of our day.

Set Up a Fish Tank

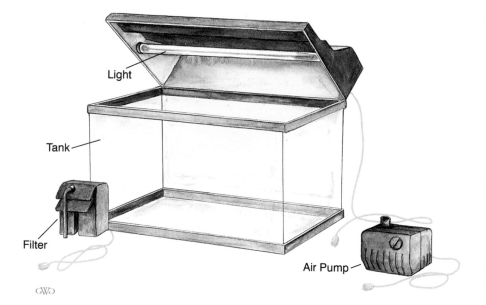

1. Go to a pet shop that sells fish. Get a tank,
   an air pump, a filter, and a light.

2. Get the tank set. Put in the pump and the
   filter. Then add sand and rocks. You may
   wish to add a small dish, a bridge, or a shell.
   Put the light at the top of the tank. Then
   fill the tank. Put a big plant in the back.
   Plug in the pump. Then the tank must sit
   for 2 days.

3. Go back to the pet shop and get fish. The pet shop has fish that are red, black, pink, and gold. Some are thin and some are fat. If a fin has a rip or cut, do not get that fish. Get some fish food.

4. Put your fish in the tank. The fish will rush* up to the top and down. They will swim in and out. They will swim under the bridge. It's fun to set up a fish tank.

* To rush is to go fast.

A Wish

subject: < **A Wish** >

To my brother,

I wish I had just one day to do what I want. This is what I would do. You and I would go on a picnic.

We would call our dog and put her in the van. Next we would fill a box with ribs, chips, and dip. Then we would put pop in a chest to chill— yes, get cold!

I want to go out to the hill. We would run to the top of the hill with our dog. Can she fetch a stick yet?

SEND

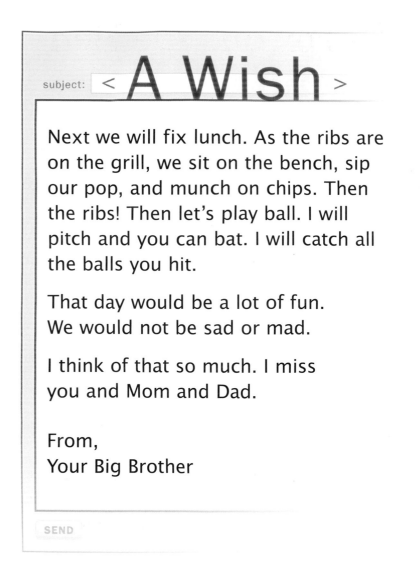

subject: < A Wish >

Next we will fix lunch. As the ribs are on the grill, we sit on the bench, sip our pop, and munch on chips. Then the ribs! Then let's play ball. I will pitch and you can bat. I will catch all the balls you hit.

That day would be a lot of fun. We would not be sad or mad.

I think of that so much. I miss you and Mom and Dad.

From,
Your Big Brother

SEND

The Fox and the Hen

This is a fox. He is very thin, but he has a plan. There is a pen with hens, chicks, and a big duck. He says, "I will rob that pen. Which hen do I want? I can catch that fat one."

When he can get the hen, he jumps into the pen. Wham! He grabs the hen. Whisk! He runs off. Whiz!

As the fox runs, the hen thinks, "Why me? What can I do? Think! Can I trick this fox?"

So the hen calls out, "Fox, why do you want *me*? I am sick. I am thin. You will not want me."

The fox yells, "Yes, I do!" When the fox yells, he drops the hen. The quick hen hops up to a branch. She sits on the branch and looks down at the fox.

"Bad luck," she calls.

Which one is the best moral?

Think when you are stuck, and
you may have luck.

Be bad. End sad.

Say much. Miss much.

A big cluck will get you luck.

Bird Bills

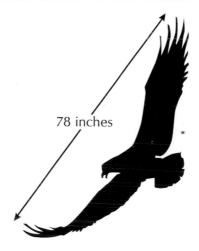

78 inches

Eagles are so big that they have a 78-inch wing span. When they stretch the wings out to fly, it is 78 inches from wing tip* to wing tip. That is as long as a tall man.

When an eagle is flying and sees a rat running in the grass, it will drop down fast and kill the rat. If you see an eagle catch a rat, you can see it ripping and cutting the rat with its bill.

A finch is small and sings a lot.

The finch gets nuts in shells. You can see it cracking the thick shell with its strong bill. The finch gets the nut that was in the shell.

The finch is 5 inches long.

*The tip is the end.

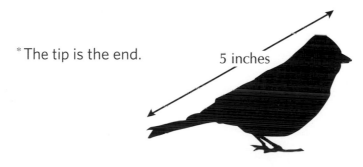

5 inches

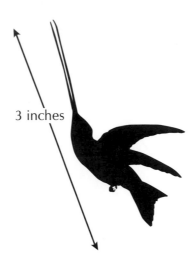

3 inches

The hummingbird is just 3 inches long. Why do we call it a hummingbird? Its wings go so fast that they hum: mmmmm.

The hummingbird has a long, thin bill. It puts its bill into a flower and sips. Its wings are going fast, but its bill stays very still.

The Dog Guide
Part 1: Ron and Lab

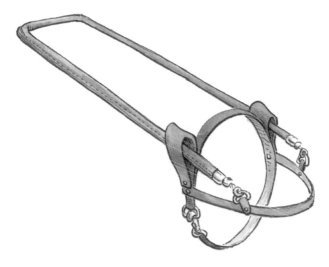

harness

Ron can not see. He has a dog guide to help him. The dog is a Lab and Ron calls him Lab. Lab sees well. He has strong hips and legs.

When Ron has to go out, he puts a harness on Lab. A harness is straps that go on Lab's chest and his back and under him.

Ron gets Lab's small rug into his pack and zips it up. He picks up his pack. He picks up the harness in his left hand. Then he tells Lab to go.

Ron and Lab walk fast. When Lab goes, Ron will go. When Lab stops, Ron will stop. If Lab sees a box in the way, he will help Ron go by the box. Lab pulls Ron out of the way so Ron will not trip or fall. That is why Lab must have strong hips and legs.

When Lab sees a dog, he will not run. He will not sniff the dog. He will not play with it. He will stay by Ron.

The Dog Guide
Part 2: To Ron's Job

Lab helps Ron go to his job. They have to cross to the bus stop. Ron tells Lab to go, but a truck is coming. Lab will not let Ron go. When the truck goes by, Ron says to go. Then Lab lets him cross.

They walk to the bus stop. When the bus comes, Lab goes to the steps. Ron and Lab step up on to the bus. Ron sits down at the front. Lab sits next to him.

When they come to Ron's stop, Lab helps Ron step down off the bus.

They walk to Ron's job. Ron sits down at his desk. He gets the rug from his pack. He puts it down flat. Lab has a long nap on the rug by Ron's desk.

No one at Ron's job will pet Lab, or talk to him, or try to play with him. Lab must stay still as Ron does his job.

Then Lab sits on Ron's lap. Ron talks to him. "You are my Lab on a lap! When I have to get a new dog guide, you will still be my pet." Ron hugs Lab.

Now Ron says, "Stand still." Ron brushes Lab with a dog brush. He pats him.

Then Ron goes to bed. He has Lab's rug next to his bed. Lab stretches and then rests on the rug.

When Lab is in his harness, he is not a pet. His job is to see for Ron. But when Lab is out of his harness, he can play with Ron and be a pet.

My Motorcycles

When I was 16 I got a motorcycle. It was old and scratched, but it ran well. I kept the tank filled, and I scrubbed it. I fixed it myself when I had to.

One day it was wet. I was going too fast. I skidded and crashed. The motorcycle was smashed, and I landed in bed till I was 17.

I missed my motorcycle. I wished for a new one. But motorcycles cost a lot. When I got well, I went to my job every day, and I did not spend much. At last I could get a new motorcycle.

The man said I could test one. I put up the kickstand, revved it up, let out the clutch, and off I went. It felt fantastic to be on a new motorcycle! I could tell it was running well.

When I got back I talked to the man. He
said he had checked it all over—the clutch,
shaft, rods, plugs, and shocks. I told him that
was the one I wanted.

I have got my new motorcycle now. As I
said, it's fantastic!

Of Dogs and Men: Two Fables

The Dog and the Ham

A dog with a ham was passing a bridge. He ran up the steps and stopped. He looked over the edge. Down in the pond there was another dog, and he had a ham, too. Dog wanted that ham.

Dog watched and watched. The other dog was still there. So was its ham.

So Dog jumped in. He landed with a splash and dropped his ham. It sank. It was lost.

But Dog could not see the other dog or its ham.

"Where are they?" he asked himself.

Moral: Too much wanted, all lost.

Two Men and the Glass of Water

Two men were sitting in the hot sand with just one glass of water. One man lifted the glass for a drink.

The other man bumped him in the chest. "Give it to me."

"Ask me," said the one with the glass.

The other man grabbed the glass and pulled. The two held on and tugged. The tugging went this way and that way. The glass slipped and dropped. The water spilled and sank into the sand.

What do you think is the moral?

Birds That Can't Fly

Part 1: The Penguin

Penguins can't fly, but they can swim as well as fish do. They use their small, thick wings. They can dive a long way down to chase fish.

On ice penguins walk, but they have small legs, so they are not quick.

Penguins have just one mate. The mother lays one egg. The male will care for the egg. He puts it on the top of his feet under a flap of skin. He stands very close to the other males so the egg will not get cold.

While the male takes care of the egg, the mother walks for one mile or more on the ice to get to the sea. There she will dive in. She catches fish and gets fat.

After 65 days the egg hatches. The mother comes back from the sea with food inside her for the chick. The chick puts its bill into the mother's bill to get the food which she spits up.

The male is quite thin now. He has not had food for a long time. He goes to the sea and catches many fish. Then he goes back to help the mother with the chick. The chick has to be fed by the mom and dad for more than 150 days.

Birds That Can't Fly
Part 2: The Ostrich

Another bird that can't fly is the ostrich.
It is larger than any other bird—8' tall. It lives
in a hot, dry land. Its food is grass and small
plants.

The ostrich will stride on its strong legs. To stride is to walk with long, fast steps. The ostrich runs fast, up to 40 mph. It sees well. It's so tall that it can see a long way and run when it has to.

When it is time for the eggs, the male will scrape a wide place in the sand. Five or more females will lay eggs in that place.

Who will take care of the eggs? The male and one female share the job. The female sits all day. She has to shade the eggs with her wings so the eggs will not get too hot in the sun. At the end of the day the male and female trade jobs.

The eggs are huge. They are more than six inches long. The shell is very thick. When it is time to hatch, the chick has to peck for two days to get out.

The chick can walk after one day. It does not have to be fed. Chicks like grass.

If an ostrich is in a safe place, it can live to be 80.

Birds That Can't Fly

Part 3: Compare* Penguins and Ostriches

* To compare is to tell what is the same and
  what is not the same.

Birds That Can't Fly

		PENGUIN	OSTRICH
1	Does it have wings?	yes	yes
2	Can it fly?	no	no
3	Places where it lives	on ice and in the sea	hot dry land
4	Size	4' tall	8' tall
5	How does it get food?	It dives into the sea and chases fish.	It bites and pecks at grass and small plants.
6	Does it make a nest?	no	The male scrapes a wide place in the sand (36 inches wide).
7	Who cares for the eggs?	The male takes the egg on his feet under a flap of skin.	In the daytime the female uses her wings to shade the eggs. Then the male trades with the female.
8	Egg care	Eggs must not get cold. They must be at 98°.	Eggs must not get hot. They must be at 98°.
9	How much time for the eggs to hatch?	65 days	42 days
10	How do the small chicks get food?	The male shares the job with the female. They spit up fish that they ate for the chick.	Chicks find grass.
11	When can chicks find their food?	when they are 150 days old	when they are 2 days old
12	What makes the chicks safe?	The male lets the chick stay on his feet.	When it is not safe, the chicks hide in the grass.

In the States

Part 1: The USA, by Pete

We have been in the USA for a while now. In the country we came from my father and mother could not get jobs. They could not vote. The country was not safe.

Now my father has two jobs. He saves a lot. We moved into a nice home.

One of my brothers is 20. He still lives with us. He works at a store and he likes his job. He brings home his pay and shares it with my father and mother. He drives now, and he votes.

My other brother is 17. He likes school very much. His grades are all fine, and he got two prizes in school.

The kids in school gave us new names. Now I am Pete.

School is OK for me. I like the kids. They help me talk in English. Every day I walk home from school with them. My mother lets me go to their homes. We talk, play games, and watch TV. We go to the mall.

I have to help a lot at home. I have to do chores (jobs) and take care of the small kids. My mom makes me do my homework.

I am glad we came here. We have a fine life now. I like American kids. I like American games and jokes. I like American life.

In the States
Part 2: The USA, by Ann

I did not want to come to the USA, but my father and mother said I had to come with them.

When we got here, I had to go to school. It was bad for me. I will tell you what I was thinking on that day.

"I am waking up. I have to go to school today. I'm scared. . . . My mother is driving me to school. I'm riding and watching the kids who are walking. I'm hating this. . . . I'm walking to my class. The other kids are staring at me. They are looking at me and watching me. I'm shaking. I want to be making friends, but I can't use English. . . . Now one of the kids is smiling at me. . . . She is sharing her snack with me. I'm hoping I can sit next to her."

School is OK now. I am liking it some. I am using English more and more. The other kids are helping me. The kids gave me a new name. Now they call me Ann. But I like my old name.

My father can not find a job using his skills (what he can do well). Every day he looks for a job, but no one is hiring. No one has a job for him. He is still hoping.

When I can get a job and save, I will go back home. Or will I like this country then?

My Fine Kids

Every time we see my grandmother, she takes out her old pictures and tells us what went on in her life.

This picture was on my wedding day. I wore a long white bride's dress and I was carrying white roses. We are just biting into the wedding cake.

We wanted a child and we had one. Her name was Rose, but she did not live long.

Then Dave came. He loved swimming, diving, jumping, running. He played all kinds of ball. Here he is running, and his father is timing him with a stopwatch. Dave did his best when someone was timing him. He liked for us to watch him.

Then we had twins: June and Rick. Twins, but not the same! No, no! June wanted to collect rocks. She got rocks of all shapes and sizes. She would spend all day finding their names in books. Here is June with a friend. Look at those piles of rocks. Every day June was trading some and saving others.

And Rick! What a child! If something was not safe, he wanted to try it. He scared me so many times. One time he went sliding down the hill and broke his hand. He went skating and broke his leg. There is his cast, and he is smiling. He went sledding and crashed.

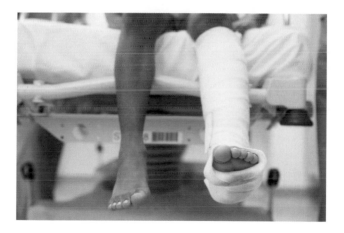

Here he is with a snake—smiling! Every day he was bringing home wild things and caring for them—bugs, frogs, fish. He loved joking. One time he put a frog down my back.

We had a fine life.

Camping Trip

tent

smoke

flames

camp

Day 1

We put up our new tents and set up our camp.
For our fire we made a ring of rocks off to the
side. No one wanted flames or smoke close to
our tents.

Day 2

We hiked* more than a mile to a lake. I went up a huge rock. I waved at my brother to come up with me. I hoped he would come up too, but he was scared. Our hike made him hot, so he just waded** into the lake. I had to take care going down the rock. My legs were so tired that they were shaking.

We were all tired at the end of the day. We had a campfire, but it smoked a lot.

* To hike is to walk a long way outside.
** To wade is to walk in water that is not deep.

Day 3

We hiked on a path that went to some huge standing stones. A man there told us that the wind had made the stones into those shapes. Some of them were standing in ponds. The water was so still that I could see the stones in it. I looked for a long time. I liked those stones.

Day 4

The sun was shining all day. We hiked over a rope bridge, down a hill, and to a store where we got lunch. Then we rented bikes and rode a few miles. I got a flat tire and had to walk back. But it was fun.

That was our last day. I hated to go home.

Hang Gliding

One day when Jane and Steve were hiking, they shared their lunch at a place where people were hang gliding. A hang glider is like a huge wing. A harness hangs under the wing, and you get into the harness.

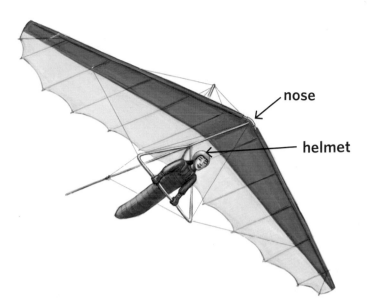

nose

helmet

Jane could not stop watching. She wanted to try it herself.

"I would be scared. Are you that brave?" Steve asked.

"I think I am," Jane said.

Steve looked at her. "You and I have hiked and skated and biked. If you care for me, don't go hang gliding."

Jane smiled. "I do care for you. Hang gliding can be safe. I will take lessons."

Steve hoped that Jane would not take lessons, but she did. Then Steve came to watch.

The place was a hill with sand and no large rocks. A strong wind was coming up the hillside. They went to the top.

Jane checked her glider and got in the harness. Then she ran down the hill as fast as she could. The nose went up and her glider left the hillside. She was gliding!

Steve watched. "What if the wind is too strong? What if the wind stops? How will she land?"

Jane glided for a while. She dipped and then let the wind lift her up. Steve could see that she liked riding the wind.

At last she landed. Steve ran over to her. Jane smiled. "Next time I want to glide where they jump off the cliff. Don't you want to come?"

"Maybe," said Steve.

Using Smell

How well do animals smell? Very well.

If you are taking care of a dog, it can tell who you are just by your smell.

Dogs can track smells. If a man is lost, let the dog sniff something that the man wore, like his socks. The dog will track that smell for miles. When the smell is old, the dog can still track it. Many times dogs have saved lost people.

Pigs (swine) smell well, too. They spend a lot of time sniffing for things they like. They can smell these things under the mud. They use their noses to dig a hole to find what they smelled.

Vampire bats smell quite well. They like to be with other bats. When a vampire bat lands next to another one, it will sniff that bat, just as dogs sniff other dogs. When they fly out looking for an animal to bite, they use their smell to find the animal.

Fish do not have noses, but they can smell:

1. Many fish live in water where they can't see. There is no sunshine down there. Smell helps fish find small fish to chase and catch.

2. A fish can smell when it is not safe. If one fish is bit, the other fish are scared by the smell.

3. Smell helps fish migrate, or swim a long way to the place where they lay their eggs.

Many animals can smell much more than we can.

Earthquakes

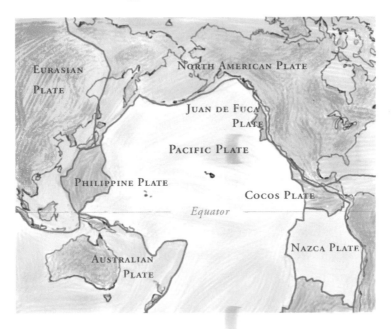

What makes the earth quake?

Under the land of the world there is a crust made of large plates that are moving.

When two plates are side by side, one is moving one way, and the other is moving another way. One edge pushes on the other. For a long time the edges stick. Then they slide, and there is an earthquake.

There are other kinds of earthquakes, too.

How strong are earthquakes?

There is a scale which tells how much the earth is shaking. A small quake is 1 or 2 on the scale. If the scale says 8, it is a very large quake.

What goes on in a strong earthquake?

The earth shakes. Some land rises up. Land can sink down. The land may crack and make huge holes. There may be landslides of mud and rocks, too.

Some earthquakes are under the ocean. They send out huge waves like walls of water. When those waves hit the shore, the water comes up onto the land.

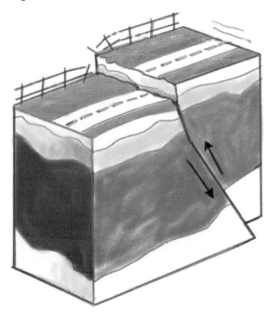

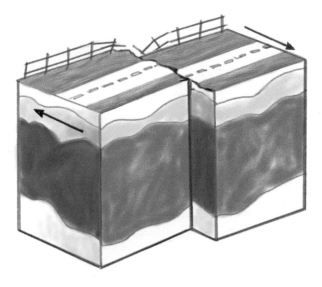

Why are people killed in earthquakes?

In most earthquakes of 7 or 8 on the scale many people are killed. If homes and buildings are not strong, they will fall down, and people can be trapped. It is not safe for others who try to get them out. If tall buildings can not flex (bend), they will fall down.

Gas pipes crack in a bad quake. After a while many fires are flaming and blazing, but people can not put them out. The water pipes are ripped, so there is no water for the hoses.

When land is hit by a wave from a quake under the ocean, the wave crushes many, many buildings.

Leeches

If you have waded in a creek or lake, you may have had a leech on your leg. A leech has a suction cup on each end. One end has three teeth that bite into your leg to make it bleed. Then the leech sucks the blood. The other suction cup keeps the leech on your leg.

Long ago people used leeches to heal, or cure, others. They thought that making sick people bleed would cure them. If a man said his head felt bad, the doctor put a leech near each ear. After a while, the doctor pulled the leeches off. The leeches did not leave cuts in the skin and the man could not feel the bite.

By the late 1800s, doctors could see that making people bleed was not a cure. Sick people were not getting well. They were just getting weak.

But leeches are back! A man's ear was cut off, and doctors put it back on. But the man's blood was not moving well through the ear. It could get in but not out. Doctors put leeches on the ear to take out some of the blood. When a leech was full, it would drop off, but blood would keep coming from the bite. That told the doctors that blood was moving. After a week, the ear was doing well. The leeches had saved it.

Doctors are now finding more ways to use leeches to heal people.

Dreams on Wheels

In the 1950s cars were sweet. People liked their look, their feel, their size, and their speed. And cars did not cost that much.

Many cars had fins, and some of the fins looked like wings. Some cars looked more like a small jet plane with four wheels. One had rear (back) fins that were more than three feet tall. Each fin had three red bulbs. When they were on, they looked like flames.

Cars came in all shades—black, white, greens, reds, creams, and more. They had lots of shining chrome on the front, sides, and rear. They had whitewall tires. People who drove the cars liked to keep them neat and shining. Many people cleaned and waxed their cars every weekend.

Cars of the '50s were large outside and inside. Three could sit in the front seat. The back seat was large, too. On a long trip kids could play in the back. No one had to have a seat belt on. There were no seat belts.

People loved their cars. In a car they felt free. They drove miles to work and to the stores. More streets were needed. People could leave home when they wanted and go east, west, to the hills, or to the beach. They wanted places to eat, so drive-ins were built. People took long trips. They needed places to sleep and get gas, too.

In the 1950s people were in love with their cars, and their dream cars gave them a new kind of life.

First Plane to Fly

In 1896 Orville Wright was very ill. His sister was his nurse. As he got well, he read how men were trying to build planes. Orville and his brother Wilbur wanted to be the first to make a plane that would fly.

The brothers watched birds and made kites. They would think, then build, then think and build, then think and build again.

In 1903 Wilbur and Orville had a plane to test. It was not very safe to test planes. The brothers chose a place with strong wind that would help lift the plane. And the place had sand to fall on.

They named their plane the Flyer. It held one man, and he had to lie down. The Flyer had no wheels. It took off from a track. The brothers hoped that the Flyer would land by sliding on the sand.

At last the day came to test the plane. The Flyer went down the track at 7 mph. It left the track, rose up just ten feet, went 120 feet, and came down in the sand. On the next test and the third test it went further. Orville and Wilbur took turns flying. On the last test the Flyer went 852 feet and stayed up 59 sec.

Late that day the brothers were going to put the Flyer in its shed. A strong wind hit the plane and turned it over and over. The plane was smashed.

Orville told his sister and father that their plane had been up four times that day. He did not say the Flyer was smashed. Orville and Wilbur were thrilled. They were the first to make a plane that would fly.

The Wright Brothers worked on these problems:

- *Would a plane be like a bird or like a kite?*

- *What wind speed does a plane need to fly?*

- *What is the best wing shape?*

- *How do you steer a plane up and down?*

- *How do you turn to one side?*

- *How do you stop the plane from rocking too much?*

- *What motor would a plane need?*

The Big Games

You may have watched the Olympic Games on TV.

The first Olympic Games were held 2800 years ago by the Greeks. There was just one race, and it was not very long: 600 feet on a track with no turns. Many fans* were there, but they were all men. No women could watch the race. After the race, speeches and feasts** went on for three days. The Greeks loved the winners.

The Greeks had the games every four years. They made the race longer and then they added more events: jumping, boxing, mule racing, and others. The games were held for a long time, but then they were stopped.

A French man wanted to bring back the Olympics. In 1896 the first Modern Olympic Games were held in the same place as the first Greek games. Many fans came to watch the first day, and not just men.

* Fans are people who love to watch games.
** Feasts are very, very large dinners.

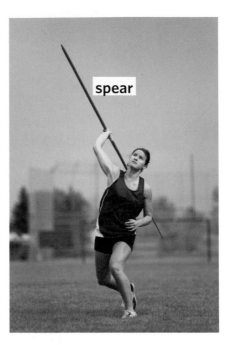

spear

The games are still going on today. Now there are both summer and winter games. At the Summer Games the athletes[***] run races, hurl spears, ride bikes, play ball games, swim, and dive. Winter games have speed skating and other events.

[***] The athletes are the people who play in the Olympic Games.

Men and women can be Olympic athletes now. Sometimes they get hurt. But they all have the same dreams: to be faster, to go further, and to do better.

Time Line

776 BCE	first name we have of Olympic winner
724 BCE	more running races added
394 CE	games were stopped
1896	first Modern Olympic Games
1900	first women athletes in the Games
1916	no Games: World War I
1924	first Winter Games
1940–44	no Games: World War II
1956	first Olympic Games on TV
1994	first Winter Games two years after Summer Games
1996	first extreme sport in Games

Sunset with the Herd

Sam looked out from under his big hat to see the sun setting in the west. The night was going to be a bad one. He could feel it in the dry, hot wind. He felt it in the dirt on his face.

"We won't have a fire tonight," he thought. "One spark in this dry wind could start a grass fire, and it would burn fast. The herd would be scared. It would be hard to stop them."

Just then, Sam saw a cow running far from the herd. He rode out fast and cut in front of the cow. He waved his arm. "Get back over there!" he yelled. The cow ran back to the herd. Sam rode back to camp.

The other men in camp were getting ready to sleep. With no fire, they ate hard bread and strips of beef. But they were used to that, just as they were used to hard work and sleeping outside in the dirt. Life out here was hard.

Sam sat down. He used to like this job. He felt free when he was outside. But now most of the time he dreamed of hot beef, hot beans, hot coffee. And a real bed. And cold clear water for his thirst.

It was getting dark. He put his head back and watched the stars, but the hot wind and sand hit his cheeks. He turned his shirt sleeves down. He pulled his scarf up and his hat down. He did not say a word, but he was thinking. "Maybe I want a job inside."

scarf

Jobs in Parks

Many young men and women spend
their summers working in parks. When the
summer is over, they go back to school.

If you can ride and take care of horses, you
could be a wrangler. Wranglers lead people on
horseback rides. They take riders to beautiful
parts of the park. During the rides they try
to keep the riders and the horses safe. They
take care of the horses by feeding them, giving
them water, brushing them, and cleaning up.

Workers on the maintenance team keep busy doing all sorts of things. If you were on this team, your job could be doing yard work or building new porch steps.

Sometimes summer storms hit the park. Then the workers pick up the branches that fell. There may be torn screens to fix. A maintenance worker's job list is not short.

Other workers meet people when they come to the park. They make people feel welcome and give them help when they need it. They give out maps, tell what the rules are, and make sure campers find the best place for their tent. At times, these workers may plan sports or other games for people to play.

These park jobs are hard, but they are in a beautiful place. When you are not working, you can hike, swim, or watch the stars. Or maybe you like to take pictures or make pictures.

Firefighters

turn-outs →

ROCKVILLE
E-32
VOLUNTEERS
"Riding With Pride"

Firefighting is not just one job. Firefighters have many skills.

When a call comes in, they have to move fast. They pull on their turn-outs. Turn-outs are thick clothes with wide stripes that shine in the dark. Their hard hats help keep them safe from fire, heat, and falling sparks.

mask

Firefighters drive huge trucks to the fire. When they get there, some firefighters pump water and aim the hoses at the building. Some raise the ladders and climb up. They use an ax to cut holes for letting the heat out.

Some firefighters have to go inside the building. With smoke masks and air tanks they find their way through thick smoke to look for people inside. They must not fail.

air
tank

After the fire is out, firefighters set up
large fans to clear the smoke out of the building.
They lift up the hoses to let the water drain*
and put them back on the trucks. Some
firefighters stay and wait to see if the fire
will start up again.

When the firefighters return, they feel
tired, but they can not rest yet. They put clean
spare hoses on the trucks. They check the
first aid kit. They get the used air tanks off
the trucks and put on full ones. Smoke and
dirt must be cleaned off the axes and fans.
When they are ready for the next call, they
can rest.

* To drain is to let the water run out.

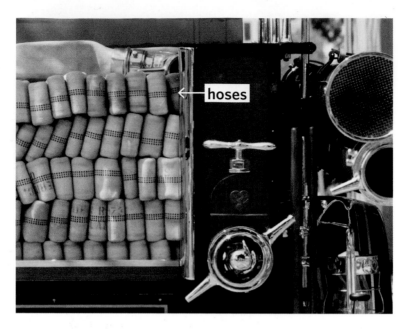

hoses

Even when there are no calls, firefighters have work to do. If dirt is left on the hoses for a long time, the dirt will rub the hoses and make holes in them. Cleaning hoses is a hard job. First the firefighters stretch out the hoses and lay them next to each other. They spray them with water and brush the dirt off with large brushes. Then they turn them over and brush the other side. They spray them again. Then they lift the hoses up onto racks to dry.

People praise firefighters for their work. Many firefighters are paid well. They are risking their lives. To do their jobs firefighters must be strong, brave, and ready at all times.

Job Hunt

Pete did not sleep well. He woke early. His father had said to get a job, but what could he do? Who would hire him? He was not even sure where to start looking. Then he thought of the library. He had heard that the library gives help on how to find jobs.

Pete walked over to the library, went up the stairs, and asked for help. The man put a website for jobs on the screen. Pete started reading.

BAIT SHOP. Part–time help needed at bait shop. Weekends only. 5:00 AM–2:00 PM.

"A bait shop?" thought Pete. "That's where people buy fishing poles. And they buy bait for catching fish. That means a lot of worms and small fish." He thought of the smell and of how early he would have to go to work. "People who fish get up too early!" Pete said. He looked at the next line.

> **PAINTER.** Paint homes with brush and spray. Start now! Fair pay.

In his mind, Pete could see pails of paint. He saw dark gray paint dripping from his brush. This job could be a mess, and he was not very neat. "I will keep reading," Pete thought.

> **WAITER.** Part–time. Must be fast. Be part of the team. Stay late weekends.

Pete would not be fast at first. Could he even carry trays of dishes? What if he tripped over a chair? What if he broke a dish? Would he have to pay for it?

Pete read down the screen.
"Wait!" he said. "I like this one!"

MAIN STREET PACK AND SHIP.
Part–time. Pack boxes for shipping.
Sort mail for rented mail boxes.
Great boss.

"No way to fail at that job! I'm sure I can do it," Pete thought. In his mind he saw the boss praise him and give him a raise. Pete left the library and got on a bus for Main Street.

Stagehand

Stagehands take care of all the props for a play. Props are the things you see on the stage—things like chairs, rugs, and plants. Anything that an actor uses on stage is a prop. If an actor walks with a cane, the cane is a prop. If an actor is to carry a tray, the tray is a prop. The stagehand's job is to put every prop in its place on the stage.

Ray is a stagehand. He gets to work early each day. Before the play starts, he makes sure that the stage is set up just right for the actors.

First, Ray looks over the stage to make sure it is safe for the actors. He does not want an actor to get hurt. One of the actors will sit in a chair, so Ray sits in it first to make sure the chair legs are strong. Next, he jumps on the stairs that the actors will walk on. He pulls on the rail to make sure it is strong. He does not want the actors to fall.

Next, Ray gets all the props in order. He has
a list of every prop that the actors will need.
One actor will carry a pail of red paint. Ray
gets the pail and sets it where the actor can
reach it. One actor will need a hammer and
nails. Ray lays those where the actor can get
them. He goes on down the list, setting each
prop in its place. The people who come to see
the play don't see Ray, but the actors thank
him for doing his job so well.

Vampire Bats

Vampire bats spend most of their time in caves, hollow trees, or cracks in rocks. There are many vampire bats crowded in the same place. They hang upside down on the walls. The only thing they eat is fresh blood.

Newborn bats are called pups. They have been growing inside the mother for 7 months, and they are born live. Bats give birth to one pup, or sometimes twins. The pups drink their mother's milk and later they drink the blood that she brings to them. The pups grow up in ten months.

Vampire bats have brown fur and no tail. They have something on the front of each wing called a thumb. When the bats are not flying, the thumbs can be like two front feet. Bats can hop like a frog or toad, and they can walk on their feet and thumbs. They can go up rock walls, too.

thumb

During the day the bats stay in. They fly out after dark. You can't hear them fly. They fly low, just three feet up. Their goal is to find animals such as cows, horses, goats, or people.

This is how a vampire bat gets blood from a cow. The bat has small pits (holes) on its face which feel heat, so the bat can tell when something warm is near. The bat can smell the cow, and it can hear the cow breathe. It can see the shape of the cow in the dark, too.

The bat lands near the sleeping cow. It walks or hops over to the cow and jumps onto it. It wants to find bare skin, so it looks for the parts with less hair. It likes the lower legs, the nose, and the ears.

Two of the bat's upper front teeth are large and very sharp. The bat pushes its head down and its teeth cut the cow's skin. It is a shallow bite, not a deep bite, so the cow does not feel the bite and doesn't wake up.

Now it's time to eat. Vampire bats don't lap like a dog or drink as we do. They don't suck like a leech. The bat sips and licks the cow's blood.

While the bat licks the blood, its saliva (spit) is running into the cut. A bat's saliva keeps the blood from clotting (drying), so the blood keeps flowing. If the bat's saliva has germs, the germs get into the animal's blood. Many animals and sometimes people die from these germs.

The bat takes so much blood at one time that it is hard to fly. It has a large load! After the bats fly back to the cave, they spit up blood for their pups. If one bat did not find blood, another bat will spit up blood for it. If a bat does not get blood for three days, it will die. Bats keep other bats alive by sharing their blood.

Soccer or Football?

It was a hot day in June. Pedro and his mother were on a bus to a Mexican town. They were going to stay three weeks with his mother's brother, his wife, and their 14-year-old, Hector. Pedro, who was just 11 years old, had been born in the US and had lived there all his life. This was his first Mexican trip. By the road, he saw farms growing rows and rows of corn and beans. The bus passed trucks carrying loads of hay. One was full of goats. The bus pulled into town just as it was getting dark. Hector was waiting for them. Pedro saw that he had grown a lot since he had come to the US last year. They walked to Hector's home, which was on the edge of town.

Early the next day, Hector got out a ball and said he wanted to play football.

"That's a soccer ball, not a football," said Pedro.

"In this country, we call soccer football," said Hector. "It's the sport we love the most. I play and I watch games. I'll take you to a game. It's great to be in the crowd."

Pedro said he was bad at soccer. "That's OK," said Hector. "I'll show you how to play. I'll be your coach. First, let's find a place to try a few kicks and passes. Most people play soccer in town."

They went to an old dirt road with no cars. It was next to a farm near Hector's yard. Hector stuck two poles into the dirt to make a goal. He then kicked the

ball to Pedro. When Pedro kicked it back, it did not go where he had aimed it. It went up in the air toward the farm and scared some crows in a tree. It came down by a brown goat and went under a cow. At last, it landed back in Hector's own yard.

Hector said, "Don't be a clown!" When he saw that Pedro's feelings were hurt, he said, "It's OK. I didn't mean it. I said I'd be your coach, didn't I? Let me show you how to aim the ball and kick it hard and low. You should kick with the side of your foot. The side is wide and will help you aim the ball where you want it to go."

"Wait, I can do this," said Pedro. He aimed at the goal. This time his kick did not fail. The ball sailed down the road, fast and low. It just missed the goal.

"Wow," praised Hector. "You sure are learning fast."

Pedro yelled back, "Wow! You are a great coach. Now the crows, goats, and cows can feel safe."

The two of them kept on playing and by the end of the day, Pedro could kick the ball into the goal most of the time. Back at Hector's home, Pedro told Hector's mother and father that Hector was coaching him to play football the Mexican way. Then he said, "Next time I'll coach Hector in football the US way."

Talking with a Go-kart Racer

How did you get started in go-kart racing?

My father was a go-kart racer, so I grew up near go-karts. On weekends we would drive to tracks in other towns and watch Pop in the races. My mother and I were in the crowd and we cheered till we were hoarse. Pop let me come down to the pit and meet the crew. I've wanted to race go-karts since I was a kid.

When I was grown, I took out a loan to buy a go-kart. It was great to go to the showroom and choose a kart.

The go-kart isn't the only cost, is it?

No, it's not. You need room to store your kart. You have to tow your kart to the track. The tracks have fees. Tools and spare parts aren't cheap. It costs a lot for food and a place to stay when you're on the road.

How did you learn go-kart racing?

My father showed me how to keep the kart in top shape and when to fix it. I learned a lot from the pit crews, too. The chain can't be too loose. Keep the clutch clean. Check the throttle. Use your slicks—that means smooth tires. But when the track is wet, use tires with grooves.

You have to learn how to drive on the track. You slow down as you come toward a turn, and speed up coming out of it. You learn how to pass. You drive to win, but not only to win. You need to be safe, too. The kart, gas, and tires heat up. You have to think of that.

Do you feel a thrill when you race?

At the start you're waiting for the green flag. The go-karts are roaring. Then your foot hits the gas throttle and you're off—boom! You start with the others, so you have to watch who's close and what they're doing. You have to think fast and keep cool.

You're riding low, doing lap after lap—vroom! You want to pull into the lead. Soon you leave the others in back. Now there are just a few in front. Then zoom—you pass the others and you win! Thrills? Yes. Winning is a thrill.

Do you have to win?

Sure, I like to win. The first time I had a lump in my throat. Winning puts me in a great mood. If you win most of the time, it's proof that you can keep your go-kart running well and you're a good driver on the track.

But I don't have to win. It's not my only goal. I like a weekend at the track. The pit crew are my friends now. I like to run a smooth race even if I don't win.

What are your plans?

First I should pay off the rest of the loan.

I'd like to own a larger kart, and that means more new tools and spare parts. And wow, there are new kinds of go-karts being made all the time.

When I was a kid I had dreams of being a big race car driver, but now I don't anymore. And that's OK.

Floating Down Rivers

Why do people float down rivers? Some like rivers that flow fast, so they choose white-water trips. "White water" means the splashing of a river that is running fast. Some people love the thrill of shooting through white water.

Others like a smooth, slow river early in the day. They watch for fish, birds, and even a turtle. They may see a duck or goose in the water, or a deer on the river bank.

Some people are on the river for fishing. They bring fishing poles, hooks, bait, and a hoop net. They put in their line and wait for a bite. When they catch a fish, they use the hoop net to scoop up the fish.

Many people float down the river on a hot day to cool off. They are in the mood to have fun in the water. They have splashing battles with their paddles. They swim for a little while, too.

Some Ways to Float

If you like white water, use a kayak. It has a top to keep out water. You sit in a hole in the top and stretch out your legs inside. There is room for one or two people, and you steer with a paddle.

paddle

kayak

white water

Many people like rafts that have room for 6 or 7. The rafts are blown up with an air pump. They have handles on the side for carrying the raft to the river. If you jump off the raft to swim, you can grab the handles to climb back on again.

One cool way of floating is to sit in the middle of a huge tube. Another great way is to squeeze the sides

of a small tube to make a kind of saddle. As you float
on this saddle, don't tip over!

Rules for Being Safe

Floating down rivers can be a lot of fun, but people can
get hurt. A few even drown. The first rule is to keep a
life vest on at all times. If people are good swimmers,
they may think they don't need a life vest. They think
it's OK just to keep their life vests in the raft or boat.
This is *not* wise. Your raft may turn over, and then it's
too late to put on the vest. If the water is very cold,
even good swimmers can soon drown.

The next rule is to watch down the river to see
where you are going. Logs and branches can be just
under water. These can rip your raft. Are you coming
toward white water? Watch for rocks that could throw
you out of the boat. Watch for other boats, too.

Some people like to float close to shore and not
in the middle of the river. You should watch for low
branches, since they can scratch you or flip your boat.

Don't let your paddle float off. You need it to steer,
and you can use the handle to help anyone who fell in
the water.

Floating on a river can be great fun, as long as
everyone is safe.

Dams

Part 1: Why Dams Are Built

A dam is a kind of wall that keeps water from flowing down a river. Some old dams are short, just one foot tall, but others are 1,000 feet tall.

People have been building dams for over 5,000 years. Why?

Dry Months

In times long ago people had to live near water. They needed water to drink and water for their cattle and crops. Many people lived where there was much rainfall. It rained or snowed through the year, so the brooks, streams, rivers, and lakes were full of fresh water. Towns were built near water.

In some parts of the world it does not rain or snow much at all. How could you live near a river that had water for only a few months every year?

Then the first dam was built. A dam keeps back some of the water in the river and makes a lake. In the months when it rains, the lake fills up. In the dry months, there is enough water in the lake for people, their cattle, and their crops.

Far from Water

Some people want to settle and live in a dry place that is far from a river. If a river has a dam, you can lay pipes from the lake to you. Water flows through the pipes to your fields, so you can grow grains and other food. You will have water for your cattle, sheep, or goats. Many large towns get their water from dammed lakes.

Floods

People living near rivers have had floods. When there are big storms with much rainfall, the water rises. It runs over the river banks, flows into houses and barns, and floods the fields. People may not see how fast the river is rising. They don't have time to move their cattle to a safe place, so the cattle drown. If the people can not leave fast enough, they drown.

A dam is a way to halt* floods. A dammed lake is kept half full. When there are big storms, the lake just fills up. You won't have floods down the river. Many lives will be saved.

* To halt is to stop.

Power

By the 1880s, there were ways to use dams to make electric power. Now one large dam can make power for many towns. Think of the lights in your home, and think of the heating and cooling you need. Think of all the cords you plug in. Where does your power come from? It may come from a dam. Wires carry the power for many miles to where people live and work.

Water Sports

After dams are built, people use the lakes for water sports. In the middle of the lake you may see boating and fishing. Near the shore, kids float in tubes and swim in the cool water. Next to the lakes are beautiful parks. You can bring food to cook or grill. You may play in the sand, or just settle back and read a good book. Many people choose to drive to the end of the lake and gaze** at the dam. It is a great sight.

** To gaze is to look at a sight for a while.

Dams
Part 2: How Dams Are Built

Any large dam takes years of planning. Why is the dam needed? What is the right kind of dam? The planners must choose the right place on the river for the dam.

Many people own land and live near the river, but after the dam is built, their land will be under deep water. Where and how will they get new homes?

It takes years to build the dam, too. Crews will be working both day and night.

Making the Site Ready

The building site is the place where the dam will be built. The building site must be dry, so first the workers must change the path of the river till the dam is built. That might be hard to do. At last, when the site is dry, the workers dig down to firm rock for the dam to be built on.

Two Kinds of Dams

Some dams are long piles of rocks and dirt. Dams must be waterproof. They must not leak. If they do, they will crumble. The rocks and dirt are pressed down so they will be very hard, not loose. Then clay or concrete is put on the outside to keep water from leaking in.

Many other dams are made of concrete. It takes months, or even years, to make enough concrete for a dam. For some dams the concrete is made at the dam site. For other dams, huge blocks of concrete are brought by truck and set on the dam with cranes.

Lake water will push on the dam, so the dam must be strong. The weight of the water is the most at the base, so the base of the dam must be much wider than the top. Water is not light!

Spillways

A picture of a dam might show water shooting out of the dam in a few places near the top. The water is coming through spillways. Spillways let water run out of the lake so the lake will not get too high.

Some spillways have gates which are like sliding doors. When the gates are closed, the lake water won't go through the spillways. After much rain, the lake might get too full, so the gates slide back and the water flows out.

Power

Dams that are built for electric power have long, steep pipes going far down through the dam. As the water starts through these pipes, it must pass through a screen. The screen keeps out fish, branches, and trash.

The water then shoots down the pipe to a turbine. A turbine is like a wheel with blades. The water falls on the blades and pushes them hard, so the turbine spins very fast. In the middle is a rod (called a *shaft*) that goes to the place where the electric power is made.

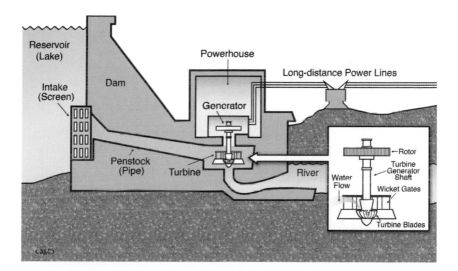

More Reading

You might like to learn more facts from books or online.

- *What are other kinds of dams and spillways?*
- *Why are taller dams best for making power?*
- *Where is the longest dam?*
- *Why is an arch dam strong?*

The Daily Mouse

News

Sunny Sky

High: sixty-eight
Low: forty-four

People Not Home

All of our readers will be happy to hear that the People, who left on their trip two weeks ago, will not be home for one more week. As you know, they took their cat and the kitty with them.

Cheese-tasting Party

A cheese-tasting party was held last week in the mouse hole of Miss J. Mouse. She had set out ten hunks of cheese.

Each mouse tasted a sample of each cheese, and then wrote down how good it was:

1. Did it taste good?

2. Was it nice to nibble?

The cheese that was voted the best was the jack cheese.

Every thirsty mouse got a cup of tea. The little ones played "Pin the Tail on the Cat" and drank punch. All thanked Miss Mouse for the party.

Meeting at School

A well-known mouse spoke to a meeting of mothers and fathers at the school last night. He brought his book, *Eating Right for the Young Mouse.* He said that kids now are eating too much candy.

"It's a simple fact," he stated. "Candy is not the food for any mouse. Look for sticky tails and noses."

Getting Well

Last month E. Mouse ran too near a knife and got a deep cut on her leg. At the sight of the blood she felt dizzy and fainted. Friends helped her back to her hole and have been caring for her since then. She is getting well now. Watch out when you are near cheese. There may be sharp knives, too.

Sports

Battle for the All-Mouse Cup

Cheering West Club fans in purple shirts turned out last night to watch their team meet East Club in a battle for the All-Mouse Cup.

East Club started the ball in play. Big M from West Club got it with his tail. He made a high curved-tail pass to Zippy Z, who shot an easy goal. East Club came back fighting, and they showed fine teamwork in making their single goal of the game.

In the biggest scramble of the night, East Club's Mighty O bit Zippy Z's tail. Mighty O was out for the rest of the half. West made one more goal as the clock was running out. It was a happy West Club crowd when the purple took the Cup!

Mouse Quiz

1. This mouse's last name was Little. He wrecked a car, but after it was fixed, he set out to find the wren* he loved. What was the mouse's first name? What was the name of the wren? Who wrote the book?
2. The Mouse King in a battle had a slipper thrown at him by a girl. Who was fighting the Mouse King? What girl threw the slipper?
3. This mouse wanted a cookie, but one thing led to another. Who wrote the book?
4. Tom and his wife got mad when the dolls' food wasn't real, so they wrecked the place. What was the wife's name? What was the name of the book? Who wrote it?
5. Name five more books or shows with a mouse.

*A wren is one kind of bird.

Bedtime Tale

Let your little mouse snuggle into bed as you read this tale.

The Tale of the Country Mouse and the Town Mouse
Long ago there was a country mouse who ate seeds from the fields near her home. Her friend lived in town and dined on cheese, bread, and jelly.

"Her food is very fine," thought the country mouse, so she took a trip to town.

Her friend led her out of the mouse hole and into the dining room. What a sight! Cake, cheese, jam and bread! She was in such a hurry that she knocked over the salt, and that woke up the cat. Just as the country mouse took her first bite, the cat leaped.

The country mouse gave a squeak of fright and ran for the mouse hole.

"This is not the life for me," she thought as she left town. "My country seeds are not as fine as cheese, but I can eat them with no cats."

Neighbors

Thursday

Dear Clare, good friend in 2-B,

It's only a month till you come back from your father's. I wish you would hurry! I'm writing to let you know what has been going on since you left.

First, it's sunny with fair skies here and a high of 75°. Is it still hot there?

Now I want you to hear all the news from here. Last week we were out front playing four square, and Ben was there. You know how he makes Kim cry? He did it again. He said she wasn't good enough to play, and she cried and went home to her mother. But her mother said, "Stop crying. Dry your eyes, and go back out." So she came back, but she didn't play. She just watched.

So the rest of us were playing, and Ben wanted to change the rules. You know Ben. When he's not winning, he tries to change the rules. No one likes it, but he still does it. Do you know Mark, that kid who's staying with his uncle in 1-D? He's tall with curly hair and freckles. Well, Mark stood right up to him and said, "No, we've started now. You can't change the rules in the middle. It's not right and it's not fair."

Ben said, "Why? We change rules all the time."

Mark said, "It's wrong. Play fair. I'm playing by the rules we started with." Then Mark served the ball. We didn't know if Ben would stay in the game or get mad and leave. But he stayed in.

Love, Kate, your friend in 3-A

Sunday

I bet you can't guess the next news. You know Mr. Bell who's on your floor in 2-A. Last month he broke his knee. Mother has been checking on him and taking him some meals. One day she fried ham and eggs and carried them down to him with toast and an apple. Well, guess who has been helping him the most? Ms. White, the woman in 3-C. She's the one who just hurries out in the morning and hurries back at night and doesn't say hi to us in the hall. She doesn't even speak to Mother and Daddy much. We thought she wasn't the kind to make friends. But she has been taking food to Mr. Bell since he hurt his knee. She cleans up his messy place and carries out the trash. Do you think they'll get married?!

Kate

Thursday

There was another party late last night in 3-B. We couldn't sleep. Mother wanted to knock on their door and try to talk to them, but Daddy said no. He said he's tried that a few times. We're tired of their parties. Daddy's going to talk to Mr. Long, who's in charge of this building now.

Kate

Sunday

A new woman has moved into 1-C. Her name is Mrs. King. She is very old and her skin is wrinkled. Mother and I went to welcome her. I can tell she will be a good friend. She said we made her feel happy to be there. She was knitting a scarf with some beautiful purple yarn. It was so soft and fuzzy. She said she would teach us how to knit! You know how we tried but couldn't do it. She will show us how to knit something simple first.

Guess what Mrs. King saves? Pennies! She has a big jar of them. She's trying to find a penny for every year since she was born. She has sixty-nine now. And Mrs. King has two little kitties, but they were shy. I couldn't get them to come out from under her bed.

Hurry, hurry, hurry back!

Kate

Photos

The people of 200 years ago stayed close to home their whole lives. They had no trains, no cars, and no planes. Most didn't have pictures, either. They didn't know what the rest of the world looked like. If you were rich, you could hire a painter to paint a picture, but most people were not rich. It's hard to think what life was like with no pictures.

Cameras Brought Changes

The first camera was made in the 1820s. For the first time, people could have pictures of their loved ones. And for the first time people found out what others in far-off places looked like. Now they could see what was going on in the world. For example, if countries

were at war, people at home could see photos showing a battle and fighting.

Pictures can be kept for a long time. Now they help us know what went on in the past. If you want to know what people's houses, clothes, work, and play looked like 100 years ago, look at old photos. If you want to see what your country is proud of, find old news photos, such as the first man on the moon in 1969.

Kinds of Cameras

There have been many kinds of cameras since the first one. Some are used to take pictures of things that are very far off, such as the stars. Other cameras can take pictures of very small things, for example a beetle.*

*A beetle is a bug.

Some cameras can be used under water, so now you can see how sharks, whales, and dolphins look as they swim. Cameras in planes and shuttles have taken photos of Earth from far off: it is a round, blue ball with swirls of white clouds.

At first cameras cost a lot and were hard to use. In the 1880s cheap cameras started to be made. They had a weight of one pound or less and were easy to use. Ever since then, many, many people have bought cameras and learned how to use them.

Taking Pictures

Some people like to take pictures outdoors. They might wait a long time for a beautiful pink and purple sunset. They might like the shapes of the clouds on a stormy day. Or they might take pictures of a bright red apple on a tree or a pretty leaf with morning dew drops. The sparkle of the sun on snow and ice can make a beautiful photo.

Some people take pictures of wildlife. They take long trips hunting for deer or eagles or bats or even leeches. When they have found one, they take shots—camera shots. Others take photos of pets. They love a dog with her young puppies or a kitty curled up on the couch. Or they take pictures of bunnies or a furry little mouse.

Many people now carry phones with cameras in them. They have their cameras ready for a good picture. Maybe their little brother is blowing a big, round bubble. Or a funny friend is putting eight large fries in her mouth at one time. Maybe an uncle tried to fly a kite. Maybe mother, father, and the kids were all dressed up, happy and smiling.

Tips

Here are some tips for taking good pictures:

- Have your camera with you all the time. You will be ready when you see a good subject. The subject is what you're taking the picture of.
- Make sure there is good light. It's best if your back is toward the light so the light shines on your subject.
- Get close to your subject so that the subject will be easy to see in the picture.
- Think of the background. The background is what is in back of your subject.
- Try to take more pictures than you will need. Then you can choose the best ones.

Laughing

Most people like to laugh: people from all countries, young and old. What is laughing? How is it good for you? Why do people laugh?

What Is Laughing?

When you laugh, sounds come out of your mouth or nose, your eyes start to close, and you may shake or rock back and forth. You breathe in more air and your heart pumps faster. You have a good feeling from head to foot.

rattle

We all started laughing very early in life. Infants first laugh when they are two or three months old. They can't yet walk or talk, but they can laugh. They might laugh at the sound of a rattle or a sound that you make with your mouth or throat. Maybe their mother shakes a stuffed bunny with floppy ears. Or their uncle blinks his eyes fast and smiles. The infant will laugh out loud and wiggle all over.

Most kids love to laugh. They like funny shows and games. Puppies and kitties are funny. Kids may have friends who make them giggle. Some read joke books and tell the jokes to each other. You may have friends who laugh at themselves. Many kids laugh just for fun. They lie down on the floor and can't stop laughing.

How Is Laughing Good for You?

Some grown-ups still love to laugh. They laugh so hard that tears come to their eyes. Grown-ups don't laugh as much as kids do. It would be better for them if they did. Laughing makes their heart stronger. It leads to other changes that help them fight off sickness and stay well. If they feel pain, laughing can make them hurt less. When grown-ups laugh, they feel less stress, so they're in a better mood.

People in every country in the world laugh, though they don't all laugh at the same jokes. Many people will laugh even when they have a very hard life with many problems.

Kinds of Jokes

What kinds of jokes make you laugh? Many people like slapstick. One example is when a clown slips and falls on his back. He tries to get up, but falls on his side. Does that make you laugh? What if the clown turns on the water and it squirts him in the eye?

Some people laugh at puns. A pun is a joke with two meanings for one word. Here are some riddles with puns.

1. What did the cat say when it fell down?

"Me-ow."

2. How do you clean a dirty bunny?

With a hair (hare) brush.

3. How many sides does an apple have?

Two, an inside and an outside.

4. The carpenter broke her tooth. How?

By biting her nails.

Some jokes are just silly.

5. How does a monster count up to 15?

On his fingers.

6. What did the nail say to the hammer?

Why don't you pound on someone your own size?

7. How can you tell when there's a bear in your sandwich?

It's hard to lift.

8. What do clouds wear in their hair?

Rainbows.

Make Up Your Own

You can make up jokes. First, think of slapstick. Let's say a clown is driving a car. Think of something funny that could happen as he drives.

Next, make up a joke with a pun. Here are some examples of words that can be used for puns: *pair* and *pear*, *wrap* and *rap*, *flour* and *flower*.

Third, can you think of a silly joke? Here is the first part: How can you tell if a bear has been in your classroom? Here is another first part: Why did the cat phone the mouse?

Country Farming and City Farming

Country Farming

When people hear the word "farm," they think of large pieces of land out in the country. Huge, noisy tractors plow the fields to get the soil ready for planting a new crop. It's better to plow when the soil is moist and not too dry and hard. But it's bad if the ground is too wet since tractors can get stuck in the mud. Right after

the ground is plowed, the farmers plant the seed and
wait for the plants to sprout. When plants are just
starting to grow, they are called sprouts. Rain will
keep the soil moist. But if there is too much rain, the
crops can spoil. A very large storm can destroy a crop.
The two biggest crops in the US are corn and
soybeans. People of all ages enjoy eating fresh sweet
corn that has been boiled in water. They roast corn in
tinfoil over hot coals, too. Corn is fed to pigs and cattle
and is even made into a kind of gas for cars.

Many kinds of food are made from soybeans.
Some people enjoy making and eating soy nuts. They
boil soybeans and then bake them to dry them out.
Soybeans are used to make soy oil for cooking food
such as French fries. Soybeans are fed to cows and
pigs and are part of the food for fish. Like corn, they
can take the place of gas. Soybeans are even used to
make a kind of wood to build homes.

City Farming

Like country farming, city farming can grow food
for people to eat. But the ground in city farming is
much smaller in size. People have found they just
need a place with some ground or some soil and some
light. You can use clay pots on shelves by windows
or on porches. Backyards are great, if your home has
one. Sometimes people even use the flat roof of a tall
building. They bring in dirt and soil.

Other people like to join a group and grow food
on school land. Girls, boys, teachers, fathers, and

mothers all work to get the soil ready, to plant the seeds, and to water and weed. When it's harvest time, everyone enjoys sharing what was grown.

There are empty places or lots where city buildings have been torn down. The city lets people rent small parts of the lot called plots of ground. People take care of their own plots.

Why Grow Food in the City?

The food grown in the city is fresh. It's better for you, since you eat it when it's ripe. And it will not spoil so soon. When there is a long way from the country to the city, the country crops are harvested when they are not yet ripe.

Growing food in the city can save you money. Many kinds of fresh food like corn, greens, beans, and peas cost quite a lot when you buy them in a store. Some people like to share their crops with others who do not have enough fresh food to eat and do not have time to grow their own food.

People enjoy growing their own food. They are proud of all the food they harvest, which can be quite a sight. They enjoy working out under a bright sun in a place where the noise of the city is not so loud.

Growing food in a city can save oil and gas and help clean the air since people do not have to make so many trips to the store. This can make the earth a better place to live.

Now you can see why more and more people want to join the growing crowd of city farmers.

Life in Antarctica

To understand Antarctica, think of a large piece of land that has thick ice over most of it. There are no trees or large plants. It is the most cold, most dry, and most windy place on earth. It has the most ice. The South Pole is in the middle, where there's no sunrise for six months. It's a long time to wait for dawn.

Cold and Dry

A summer day in Antarctica seems hot if it's higher than 32°. In winter, it has got down to -128°. Try not to freeze your eyes shut when you breathe. The moist air from your lungs causes ice to form on your mouth, nose, and eyes. If you spill a cup of water, the water will freeze by the time it hits the ground. What can live in such a cold place?

Living All Year in Antarctica

The only animals that can live all year in Antarctica are very small bugs and worms. Think of a worm less than one-sixteenth of an inch long. In the summer, when melted ice makes the soil moist, this worm can eat and move. When winter comes, it dries out and coils up. It does not move for nine months until the ice thaws* and makes the soil moist again.

* To thaw means to melt.

Part-time on Land and Part-time on Ice

Some animals live on Antarctica part of the year. Some penguins hatch and raise their chicks on the winter ice and snow. They stand close to each other to keep from the cold and wind. The claws on their feet keep them from slipping on the ice when they are standing and walking. When they slide on their bellies, they push themselves with their feet. Their claws grip the ice and make them go faster.

Seals come to land to give birth to their pups. They haul themselves out of the water using the claws on the front of their flippers. They haul themselves out to enjoy a rest after feeding, too.

It's too cold for flying birds to stay in Antarctica for the winter, but a few lay their eggs there in summer.

There are no plants large enough for building a nest, and there is no place to hide the chicks. These birds lay eggs on the ground. They stay close to chase off other birds that might destroy the chicks.

Sea Life

There is not much life *on* Antarctica, but the seas that surround it are full of life: whales, dolphins, seals, penguins, fish, and krill.

What are krill, and why do they matter? Krill are like shrimp. Each one is only two inches long, but there are millions and millions of them. They are the food for much of the other sea life.

For example, blue whales eat krill. A blue whale can be 100 feet long. It has no teeth. How does it eat enough krill to fill its belly? On its large upper jaw it has many plates hanging down. The plates are like large fingernails. They are strong, but they can bend. The whale drops its bottom jaw and takes in water and krill. It closes its jaws, causing the sea water to flow through the plates and out its mouth. The krill are left in its mouth. A blue whale can eat hundreds of pounds of krill a day.

blue whale

Many seals eat krill, too. With jaws wide, they fill their mouth with water and krill. When they close their jaws, water is strained out through their teeth. All the krill are trapped inside.

As you know, whales, dolphins, seals, and penguins have to come to the top of the water to breathe. How can they live when the winter ice forms over the sea water? Most of them will not swim near the winter ice. But one seal, the Weddell seal, can make holes in the thick ice. Its front teeth are set in its jaws so that they can scrape ice, so this seal scrapes breathing holes for itself. It knows where its holes are, and it can keep scraping off new ice that forms, so that the hole won't close.

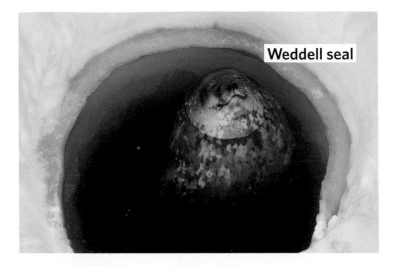

Weddell seal

The wildlife in Antarctica is fantastic. Many countries in the world have joined in making laws to keep it safe.

Lost

It was late on a cold, windy afternoon. Father was sure it would snow by night.

"Do your chores early," he said to his sons. "We'll get the work done and be safe inside for supper."

James and Paul knew their jobs. They had to milk the cows and carry fresh water from the well. It was hauling the water that caused the fight. James said it was Paul's turn, and then James teased him.

"Do I annoy you?" James asked. "Are you mad, little brother?"

The fight started. James held Paul down tight on the floor. With all his strength Paul threw James off and ran out the barn door. He was hot from fighting and mad, too. He ran straight into the dark woods that surrounded the farm. Paul was so mad that he didn't think what he was doing or where he was going.

Paul ran on. Snow started falling, and the flakes cooled his head. At last he slowed down to a walk. After a while he didn't feel so mad. He knew he should go back now. Father would expect the chores to be done, and Mother's hot supper would be waiting in the house.

Paul turned and started back. He felt cold. He walked a long way, but he couldn't see Father's fields or buildings through the trees. Paul paused. Where was home? He was lost.

First Paul thought he could follow his tracks home, but the snow was filling his footprints fast. Then Paul thought of what his father had said to him once: "Son, if you get lost, stay where you are. Don't go further. Stop and wait."

OK, he would stop and wait. Father and Mother would miss him soon, and James would tell them that Paul had run off. What would they do? They might think that Paul would come home when he wanted to. They might not know that he was lost. Would they come looking? Maybe they couldn't start till dawn.

Paul was very cold now. His fingers and toes did not have much feeling. He had to think of a way to keep warm. There were some pine trees near him with soft needles. Paul broke off as many branches as he could. Then he crawled on the ground getting old leaves from under the snow, and he made a pile. He sat down on the leaves and leaned back on a tree. Then he pulled the pine branches over him. This was better than standing in the wind.

Paul thought of home, Mother, Father, and James. Why did Paul fight with James? It seemed silly now. What did it matter whose fault it was? Why did he run into the woods? He could have been home eating supper. Why did he have to spoil it all?

The only noise he heard now was the blowing of the wind. Once he read a story of a girl in haunted woods. He tried not to think of that story now. He needed to wait until dawn. When it was light, maybe he would know what to do next.

Paul yawned. He felt sleepy. He slept, but he had bad dreams. In one dream a hawk flew over him again and again. It was trying to destroy him. Then his brother was pointing at him and laughing. Then he dreamed that he sat down to a large supper and just as he picked up his fork, all the food spoiled.

Paul woke up. The wind and snow had both stopped. He was still very cold, and he hurt all over. All of a sudden he heard a noise from far off. It sounded like a shout. Paul got to his feet. He saw a small light through the trees. Paul yelled as loud as he could. "Here, come here!" He wanted to run toward the light, but his legs were too cold and stiff.

"I'm here!" he shouted again.

The light grew larger. It was coming toward him. He saw Father, Mother, and James hurrying through the snow.

Mother hugged him tight with tears of joy. Father looked at the leaves and branches Paul had built up. "Well done, son," he said.

Father led the way, while Mother and James helped Paul walk. They went back through the woods toward home.

Dress Codes

Many schools have dress codes. A dress code is a set of rules for what students may and may not wear to school.

What Do Dress Codes Say?

Most dress codes start by saying that all students must be clean and neat. Clothes may not have holes in them or be messy. Clothes must be neither too tight nor too loose. Pants with belt loops must be worn with belts. Students may not wear anything over their faces.

Neither skirts nor shorts may be too short. Students may not wear see-through fabrics such as lace. Shoes must be worn, and that means that toes cannot be seen. Some schools do not let students wear jeans, and in most schools students can't wear T-shirts with words or pictures that insult others.

Dress codes have many good points. A good point is called a *pro*. When people say that dress codes are bad, they are thinking of the cons. Let's look at the pros and cons of dress codes.

The Pros of Dress Codes

Why have dress codes? Some people think that dress codes solve many problems. When students' clothes are clean and neat, everyone can concentrate on their school work and not spend so much time looking at each other's clothes. Some people say that grades go up in schools with dress codes. Students feel proud of themselves and their school.

Some people feel that dress codes help students get ready for the jobs they will have when they grow up. When men and women look for jobs, no one wants to employ them if their shoes and clothes are messy or dirty. Dress codes help students dress for success.

Many people think that students should wear uniforms, such as a white shirt with blue shorts, pants, or skirt. When students don't have to think of which clothes to buy and wear, they can spend more time on school work.

Another pro of uniforms is that students don't judge one another by their clothes. When everyone dresses in the same outfits, you don't hear students saying, "Your blouse is so pretty! I wish I had one like that." With uniforms, students will be judged on how they act, not on what they wear.

When schools have uniforms, many fathers and mothers are glad that they can save money on school clothes. Clothes prices can be very high. When you don't have to spend money on fancy clothes for school, you have more for other needs.

The Cons of Dress Codes

Some people think that dress codes are wrong. They say that dress codes don't cause students to get better grades or act better.

They say that dress codes are trying to make everyone the same. Schools should be saying, "Be yourself. Find out who is the real you." Dress codes keep kids from finding their own voices. It's good for young people to think of what kind of people they want to be and show who they are to the world. They need to learn to make choices.

Some students say they have a right to wear and enjoy the clothes they want. If they have bought clothes that are nice, pretty, fancy, or even ugly, they have a right to wear them.

Some students know that their clothes annoy their mothers, fathers, and teachers. They say it's fine for grown-ups to give advice on clothing choices, but they don't want dress codes to force them to wear uniforms.

One con of dress codes has to do with students' faiths. In this country we can join any faith we want.

In some faiths men and women wear a kind of hat or head scarf. Telling students not to wear the clothing of their faith is a problem.

Your Thoughts?

When schools and students don't think the same way on dress codes, they can ask a judge to rule on the law. Now there are laws on dress codes, but there is still a lot to say.

What are your thoughts on the pros and cons of dress codes? Are uniforms best for schools? Should there be the same dress code for grade schools, middle schools, and high schools? Can you think of some new points to make?

Mountain Lions

Mountain lions are big, wild cats. Not so long ago, there were very few mountain lions left. What was the cause? People were killing as many as they could. Farmers didn't like mountain lions eating their sheep, horses, and cattle. Now many states enforce laws that say you cannot kill mountain lions. The number of the big cats is growing.

What Mountain Lions Look Like

ntain lion coats are light brown and their ears and
ve black tips. They have some black and white

markings on their faces. The cubs have black spots on their brown coats.

When full-grown, they can be up to eight feet long. The male has a weight of 110 to 180 pounds, and a female, 80 to 130 pounds.

How Mountain Lions Live

Mountain lions can be found all over the West. A small number of them live in the far South. They like to be on their own. Only females who have cubs live in groups. Mountain lions live twelve years in the wild, but can live much longer in zoos.

When the females give birth, they have from two to four cubs. The mother raises them without help from the father. The cubs nurse for eight weeks, and then the mother starts teaching them how to hunt. Cubs stay with their mother for up to two years.

Mountain lions are big animals and they eat a lot, so they need a lot of space for hunting. They walk a long way when looking for food. The number of miles they go when hunting is called their *range*. Mountain lions have ranges from 60 to 100 square miles.

Many mountain lion cubs don't live long, but those that do must find their own ranges. When they leave their mothers, young mountain lions go out looking for their own hunting grounds. These young lions can spend up to a year looking for a home range. Like other young animals, many will make mistakes. They might make too much noise while hunting and not get enough food. They might be caught by a hungry bear. If a young mountain lion succeeds in finding its own range, and if it hunts well enough to fill its belly, it will survive. It will live.

What Mountain Lions Eat

Mountain lions will eat any animals they can catch, even mice, which for them are a nice snack. Their first choice, though, will be deer and elk.

These big cats hunt at sunset, at night, or at dawn. They walk without making a sound, and they can leap 15 feet high and 40 feet long. They like to live in places with lots of trees so they can hide. They are very good at waiting for just the right time to pounce.

To kill a deer, they leap onto its back. They have jaws that are just the right size to fit onto the back of a deer's neck. The bite kills the deer very fast. Then the mountain lion eats as much of the raw meat as it can. If a mountain lion mother has cubs, she lets them join her to eat.

The mountain lion doesn't eat the whole deer at once. When its belly is full, it digs a hole in the ground. It drags the rest of the deer into the hole, and then paws leaves over the meat to hide it. It wants to make sure there are no signs of food that other animals can find. The mountain lion comes back for more meals. One kill is enough for many days. But sometimes another animal, like a bear, finds the kill and eats it.

Mountain Lions in the City

Sometimes mountain lions make their way into cities. Most of the time, people never see any sign of the big cats. They are very shy. They don't want to be seen. The only sign they leave is their tracks.

A mountain lion track is very big, three to five inches long. It is bigger than the tracks of most dogs. The way to tell if a track was left by a dog or a mountain lion is to look for the claw marks. When cats walk, they keep their claws in. Dogs cannot do that. So dog tracks have small points or holes at the top of the pad marks and mountain lion tracks do not.

Large Dog   **Mountain Lion**

There are very few cases of mountain lions attacking people. In fact, deer, who can kick hard, kill many more people than mountain lions do. Even bee stings kill more people than mountain lions do.

The Race to the South Pole

If you look at a globe and see the part as far south as you can, you will be looking at Antarctica. The South Pole is near the center.

No one knew that Antarctica was there until 1820. Over the years people wanted to explore Antarctica. They sailed there and made maps of the coast. They found that the seas are the most stormy in the world. When they explored inland, they found that there is ice on most of Antarctica. Antarctica is the most cold, most windy, and most dry place on earth.

By 1900, no one had yet been to the South Pole. The pole is near the center of Antarctica, and that is 800 miles from the coast. Explorers wanted to be first to reach the Pole. People at home were proud of their own country, and they wanted explorers of their country to be first. It was exciting to think of a race to the pole.

Planning for the Trip

The trip would take three months, and the cold and wind would be extreme. There was a chance that any trip would fail. There were two men, though, who very much wanted the fame of winning the race to the South Pole. One was Scott, an English man. The other was Amundsen of Norway.

Both leaders planned with care. They needed clothes and boots for the extreme cold. They would have to keep their faces from freezing. They would carry small stoves to heat food and melt ice for drinking water.

Tents would be their only shelter, so they needed tents that wouldn't rip or be blown over by the strong force of the wind. The best way to haul their food and tents was by sledge. A sledge is a large sled that can carry great weight.

Amundsen and Scott set up camps in Antarctica in 1911, but far from each other.

Slow and Fast Paces

Scott tried dogs and horses for hauling sledges, but he felt that the best choice was for the men to do the pulling. His group started for the Pole. Others went with them at first to store piles of food which Scott would need on the way back. The men found that hauling the sledges was hard work, and their pace was slow.

The group from Norway had brought dogs to haul their sledges, and the dogs had been trained to pull sleds in the cold. Amundsen went part of the way, leaving piles of food and oil, and then came back for more. He knew he could keep a faster pace if the sledges were light. So he planned to kill some dogs on the way as food for the men and other dogs.

The Pole

Amundsen's team started for the Pole. Two months later, they reached it. No one else had been there. Amundsen put up a flag from Norway and wrote a letter to Scott. Then he left. The men made it back to the coast, and they sailed home to tell the world that their trip had been a success. They had won the race.

Scott and his men reached the South Pole 34 days after the group from Norway. They had succeeded in getting to the Pole, but they hadn't won the race.

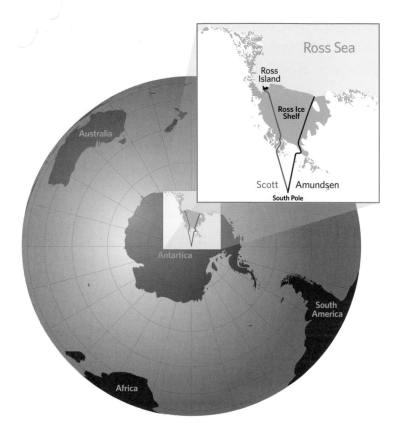

Scott's Trip Back

Scott's team started the 800-mile trip back, but they were very tired and their food would soon be gone. First one man died. A snowstorm struck and they had to stay in their tents for days. Another man died.

The men were just 11 miles from a food pile when a snowstorm hit again. They lay in their tents day after day with the noise of the wind. They grew weaker. At last they died.

Months later they were found. Scott had been writing in a book each day to tell of their struggle. He wrote even when he knew he was dying.

After the Race

So twice in 34 days men had reached the South Pole. No one went there again for many years. Both leaders gained world fame, but people talked of the two trips. What were the true causes of Amundsen's success, and why did Scott fail? Was Scott at fault, or was he just not lucky? Did he ignore good advice? For more than 100 years since then, people have wanted to know.